The Story of You

by Sheila Griffiths

PRIMA PJ

Published in 2014 by Prima PJ

ISBN: 978-0-9929691-0-3

Photographs sourced through Foter.com and istockphoto.com. Cover design by IAS.

Dedication

The book is to James, Hazel and Martin

Acknowledgements

I would like to thank my family for their love and support. I am also really grateful for the time they each gave to read my drafts. I would also like to thank my editor Christine McPherson for all her help and encouragement. Most of all I need to thank Kim and Sinclair Macleod of Indie Authors Scotland for without them this book may never have been published. They have been a font of knowledge and friendly guidance throughout.

Introduction

We all have different paths to travel to reach our potential for health, wealth and happiness. Sometimes you can become lost, and life can seem unbearable. I have written this book to help you. Realising the power of your mind will help you to find your path through life and all it throws at you. I first became interested in the mind many years ago when I started an adult class for psychology, and eventually went on to gain an Honours degree in the subject through the Open University.

During my study, meditation was often mentioned on the course, but not in any great depth. However, it sparked my interest and I began to read about meditation, then learned to meditate myself.

When my daughter and her family emigrated to Australia, I found my life had completely changed. And this made me realise how easily my thoughts were able to make me feel unhappy. I read books and internet articles about the power of the mind and our ability to be in control of our thoughts.

I began to realise that if I could stop my thoughts running amok, I could be in control and decide the actions I should take to make my life better in all areas.

My studies helped me become more understanding of my mind and helped me through what was a very difficult time. And the realisation that I needed to share this information with others led to the creation of this book.

Please take the hand I offer and let me help you back to your true path through life.

YOU
in the Beginning

Here you are, reading this book. Why? You have been drawn to it. You are meant to be here. Perhaps when you have read it, you will understand why; or perhaps not. You may not yet be ready, though, and may need to read it again when you feel you are more open to new thoughts and willing to let go of negativity.

It doesn't matter whether you are young or old, rich or poor, male or female. It doesn't matter your nationality, the colour of skin you have, or if you have a religion or not. This book is for you.

This is the story of you. You began when one male sperm entered a female egg and nature allowed you to exist. The body in which you grew could have rejected you, but it didn't. Instead, it nourished you and allowed you to develop, until you were ready to come out into the world and breathe by yourself; able to grow, learn and achieve, with everything you needed to reach your full potential and achieve your purpose in life.

Have you found your purpose in life and reached your potential? Are you happy with the life you have? If not, why not? After all, if you were born with the ability to reach your full potential, why haven't you?

YOU
and Breathing

No matter how bad you feel your circumstances are at this present time, you can start by appreciating the simple fact that you can breathe. Without breath, there is no life.

Breathe deeply and relax.

Breathing is the one thing that everyone has to do. Most people shallow breathe, but your lungs, heart and brain prefer deep breathing, as more oxygen can then circulate and make them work more efficiently. The deep in-breath will cleanse, and the long out-breath will clear.

By concentrating on your breathing, you can learn to master your mind. Simply sit, relax, concentrate on your breathing, and let your thoughts drift away. Do not follow them, just let them go.

If you find it hard to concentrate the mind and stop it wandering off, try saying the word 'cleanse' on the in-breath and the word 'clear' on the out-breath.

Stretch the words 'cleanse' and 'clear' as you take deeper breaths in and longer breaths out. In this way, your mind is made to focus on your breathing. And with your mind clear and focused, you will be able to absorb what you are reading.

As soon as you realise your mind is wandering off again, bring it back by concentrating on your breathing and this will put you back in control.

YOU
and Thinking

B reathe deeply and relax.

Isn't it amazing the amount of thoughts your mind can produce? But that is what your mind does.

All day long it produces thoughts, and it is up to you to decide which ones you hold onto, and those you let go.

Your thoughts can be good or bad, positive or negative; your mind doesn't differentiate. It just produces thoughts. It's up to you which ones you choose to follow.

The only things holding you back in life are your thoughts.

So take time to understand how thoughts form and accept that this is all they are – just thoughts. They won't affect you unless you act on them, so choose wisely which thoughts are worth acting on.

Try to take time each day to just sit comfortably and relax, and concentrate on your breathing. Notice the thoughts that come into your mind, but do not stay with them. Just accept they have formed, then let them go.

When you become more aware of your thoughts, they will stop having such a hold on you, and you will become more aware of what is happening around you.

Breathe deeply and relax.

YOU
Can Smile

Photograph courtesy of Tambako The Jaguar

B reathe deeply and relax.

Smile.

No matter how good or bad you think your life is at this moment, just smile. It will send a feel-good message to your brain.

Smiling can also be contagious and spread to others.

If you feel you can't smile, grip a pen lengthways between your teeth. This will give your mouth the right shape and make the brain think you are smiling. If you physically can't smile for some reason, visualise yourself smiling.

A smile is the first step in feeling good, and what better way to continue?

Smile each day and it will draw others to you.

It is also good exercise for your face.

A real smile which makes the eyes sparkle will not only make you feel better, but all those around you will feel the effect of a true smile.

That same smile could brighten someone else's day as well as your own, and you might never even know; they may just have caught your smile in the passing.

Breathe deeply, relax – and smile.

YOU
Can Relax

Photograph courtesy of John Fowler

Breathe deeply and inhale all the way down into your abdomen, with a long exhale. And relax.

Let the tip of your tongue rest against the roof of your mouth just behind your front teeth. Your lips will part slightly and you will have a gentle smile on your face relaxing the muscles in your jaw.

Close your eyes tightly, then open them, and feel your forehead and the rest of your face relax.

Make tight fists with your hands, and bring your shoulders up towards your ears. Then drop your shoulders, release your fists, and let your neck, shoulders, arms and hands relax.

Tense up your pelvic floor, abdomen and chest, and then relax all the muscles in your body. Feel all your muscles relax.

Bend your feet up so the toes are pointing towards your body and the back of your legs are stretched.

Now release the feet and let the muscles in your legs relax.

Curl your toes tightly and then let them relax.

From the tip of your toes to the top of your head, you should be completely relaxed. If necessary, repeat the steps until you feel you are relaxed.

YOU
are Here and Now

Photograph courtesy of Sinclair Macleod

Breathe deeply and rhythmically, and remain relaxed.

Today is the first day of the rest of your life. This very moment is precious; you have this moment only once. Be aware of, and be happy in, this present moment.

As you are reading these words, let only these words be in your thoughts. Let no other thoughts bother you at this moment in time.

Breathe deeply, smile and relax.

The present is where you should be. You cannot change the past, and the future is yet to come. Enjoy the here and now, and appreciate this moment in your life. Concentrate only on the words you are reading. It is *your* mind, *your* body, and *your* decision whether you relax and continue to read or not.

You are where you are today because of the

thoughts you decided to follow. What you think about, you bring about. You can choose to continue to live your life this way, or you can choose to change. The choice is always yours and no-one else's. So first, you need to realise what it is you are thinking.

Breathe deeply and relax.

YOU
and Happiness

Photograph courtesy of Angell Williams

You may be reading this book, or having it read to you, in a search for happiness. But you need to know that you never lost the ability to be happy. It has been within you all the time.

Don't look to others, or material possessions, for your happiness. Nor will you find it with excesses of food, sex, drink, or drugs.

Stop thinking you can only be happy when the perfect man/woman comes into your life, or you have enough money, or own the newest car, house, or latest gadget.

Happiness is within you, and it is just waiting for you to let it through. Not tomorrow or next week, or next month, but now. This very minute, there is nothing to stop you from feeling happy, except you and your thoughts.

You will be as happy as you make up your mind to be. You are only ever one thought away from changing your life.

Breathe deeply and relax.

This is your time to clear away negative thoughts. The more negative thoughts you have, the more negativity you will attract into your life, and the more you will suppress your happiness.

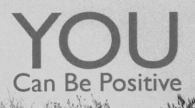

YOU
Can Be Positive

Photograph courtesy of Philip Leara

You attract into your life what you think most about. It is worth repeating, 'You are where you are today because of the thoughts you chose to follow', if it helps you to understand the power of your thoughts.

Try to be aware of your thoughts at all times. What are you thinking just now? If you find it's a negative thought, try changing it to a positive thought. If it's a positive thought, well done.

Stay relaxed and continue to breathe deeply. Your thoughts can be very hard on you at times, saying things to yourself you would never say to others. For example, sometimes your thoughts may say you're ugly and stupid. As soon as you realise you are thinking this way, you need to change your thoughts by telling yourself the opposite: you are beautiful and clever. And feel it, believe it. Become your own best friend. Learn to love the real you, and stop finding fault with yourself.

Let only positive, happy thoughts take hold in your mind. Remember, everyone is beautiful in their own way. We each have different talents to share with the world. No one person is better than another.

And you deserve to be happy. It is your right. Life is for living, loving, and making the world a better place for everyone and every living thing.

So where are your thoughts now?

Breathe deeply and relax, and come back to the words in the book.

YOU
Can Achieve

B reathe deeply and relax.

You are special; there is no-one else like you.

Do not let anyone tell you otherwise, not even your-self.

You have everything you need to achieve what you want to achieve. If you have not learned to notice the influence your thoughts have, they will have great power over you – especially your subconscious – and stop you from being happy, and reaching your full potential in life.

It is like living on autopilot, unaware of the opportunities that come into your life or the kind of life you could be living.

Breathe deeply and relax

If you really want to, you can take back full control of your life by learning to be mindful of your thoughts and emotions. (Emotions are a good indicator of whether your thoughts are happy, sad, etc.) No-one else can make you mindful of your thoughts, only you can. So if you want to have control of your life, to live a happy, contented, healthy life, only you can decide if you want to change.

You are the one who chooses whether you are happy, or sad. Happiness is always within; it's just waiting for you to let it through.

Breathe deeply and relax.

Life is a journey and it's up to you which path you choose. You can choose to walk a well-worn path and be led by others, or you can set out to create your own trail. Whichever way you choose, it is your own personal path, suited to you. Do not compare yourself to others. Everyone is different and each has their own path to travel.

Breathe deeply and relax.

Ask yourself what is it you really want to achieve then visualise yourself having achieved it. Feel it. Really feel what it is like to achieve your goal. Visualise it clearly. In what way will your life be different? Where will you be? Who will be with you? Then ask yourself what steps you can take now towards achieving that goal.

Become more aware, and look for opportunities

that may lead to your goal. But don't cause suffering to others to reach your goal, as that will prevent your achievement from being worthwhile and you will not find contentment in your success.

Sometimes, however, you have to move on and leave others behind to achieve your potential. This can be done by making sure any responsibilities are safely taken care of.

Breathe deeply and relax, and bring your thoughts back to now.

YOU
Can Regain Control

photograph courtesy of Sam Howzit

B reathe deeply, relax and keep smiling.

Let your thoughts come and go. You can't stop your mind thinking, but you now know you don't have to go along with the thoughts. Just appreciate the wonder of the mind and watch it at work. Let each thought form, then let it go. It is only a thought. It does not mean anything and cannot affect you, unless you allow it to. Just let it pass.

Breathe deeply and relax.

The untrained mind is like an unused muscle, so you will need to practise every day to improve and be aware of your thoughts. You may find your mind races, and your body tenses.

If your mind is really racing and unwanted thoughts play over and over again, it can help to put one hand below your nose and feel your breath on your skin, as you concentrate on your breathing.

Relax the body and just be the observer of your thoughts. Do not let the mind wander off and go with the thoughts.

Let the thoughts go, stay relaxed, and concentrate on your breathing. The more you practise this over time, you will find that your thoughts will slow down. In time, you may even achieve gaps between your thoughts. That's fine. Just enjoy the wonderful relaxed feeling that comes from not chasing after your thoughts.

You are in control. You will learn at the speed that suits you, so do not compare yourself with others.

Breathe deeply and relax.

If someone says something insulting to you, it cannot hurt you unless you let it. Don't allow it to stay in your mind, playing over and over and making you miserable. Instead, let it pass. Let it go. This person has a problem with their own thoughts, if their only way to make themself happy is to try to hurt others. Do not be like them.

The more you think negatively of yourself and others, the more negativity you will draw into your life, including ill health. Ill health thrives on negativity and stress. If you always look for the good in others and in life, you will find more good things come your way.

Don't say every day that you hate your work, your body, your life, etc. It will only make you feel worse and attract more of the same. Instead, look for something good – no matter how small. And if you cannot find anything, then imagine something good. The more you tell yourself you are happy and enjoying your work or life, and visualise and feel happiness, the more good will come into your life and good things will happen.

Breathe deeply and relax.

You attract into your life what you think most about.

You may in time find yourself guided to what is the perfect job, partner, or house for you, and to attain the life designed for you, as everyone is different.

So long as you have daily food, a roof over your head, and the love of others, then you have everything you need and are richer than you think.

Do not keep comparing yourself to others, or coveting what they have. Just be happy being you.

Breathe deeply and relax.

YOU
Can Reach Your Potential

Where are your thoughts now? Bring them back to now by breathing deeply, then smile and relax.

You may wonder why you have not yet reached your potential, and think negative things about yourself and others. Perhaps you have reached a good place in life, but you haven't noticed because you still want more.

Not reaching your potential comes from the beliefs you have learned from childhood and which are buried in your subconscious.

When you were a child, you were surrounded by people who were probably only trying to do their best for you; or perhaps not. Whether it was family, friends, teachers, or others, they did not know they needed to speak to you positively and nourish your growing mind, and to avoid putting you down with disparaging remarks or actions.

You may have allowed yourself to believe their criticisms, and held onto the negative thoughts and emotions you experienced, eg, they may have said you're stupid, you're lazy, you will never amount to anything, you don't deserve any better, etc. If you persisted in taking in these negative comments over and over again, they would have become embedded in your subconscious mind, because we learn by repetition.

Breathe deeply and relax.

You will unknowingly be living your life according to these limiting beliefs which were taken on board as a child and buried in your subconscious mind.

Without being aware of how these beliefs have influenced you, you will always have found excuses for why you couldn't do something, ignored your intuition, and never reached your full potential.

You need to be aware that unless you correct these limiting beliefs, they will continue to hold you back from being the best you can be. These thoughts can also be enforced later in life if you become involved with friends and acquaintances who constantly put you down and surround you daily with negative thoughts.

Breathe deeply and relax, and let any tension go.

You need to correct what you believe about your-self. Choose positive affirmations about yourself and repeat these two or three times to yourself every day. Really feel and believe them.

However, make sure you do not say what you do *not* want, eg. I don't want debt; I don't want to live in a rundown house; I don't want headaches. The mind will just grasp onto the words you use and give you more of it – more debt; more poor housing; more headaches.

The mind does not differentiate between good and bad, it just gives you whatever it is you focus on most.

You have to make statements about the 'you' that you want to be. For example: every day in every way I am getting better and better; I always maintain a healthy body, mind, and immune system; money comes to me easily and frequently; I am always kind and caring and attract others to me; I have a wonder-ful family, fabulous house, and fantastic car.

These have to be your affirmations and should be in the present tense, as if you already have them. Don't just say them; visualise and feel what it would be like to be this way. You are out to convince your subconscious that what you say is already true.

Breathe deeply and relax while you visualise.

Really think about what you want your perfect life to be like.

Write your affirmations down, if you prefer, and as you repeat them each day and really feel they are true, you will begin to memorise them and they will become part of your subconscience.

Try to aim for about twelve affirmations, covering the different areas of your life – samples are given throughout the book – and repeat them until you remember them passionately. It is important to feel real emotion, to really feel what it would be like to have the life you want.

Remember, you learn by repetition.

Given time and constantly repeating your affirmations, you will find your life changing for the better.

To help attract more good things into your life, start each day by being grateful for everything you already have then repeat your affirmations.

Be grateful for all the small things in your life that you probably take for granted each day, i.e. food on the table; clothes on your back; the ability to see, hear, feel, taste and touch; the clean water from the tap; electricity at the flick of a switch; the sun, wind, rain that helps the crops to grow, etc.

You will be amazed how good your life really is. You just have not ever taken the time to notice.

Breathe deeply and relax.

Photograph courtesy of James Jordan

Photograph courtesy of William War

Photograph courtesy of Bureau of Land Management, Oregon

YOU
and Emotions

Photograph courtesy of Nikos Koutoul

B reathe deeply and relax.

There will be times when you feel sad or angry, but that is alright. Without sadness, how would you know happiness? Without anger, how would you know peace? Without stress, how would you know you are relaxed?

The important thing is not to let these negative emotions take over, but to recognise them and acknowledge them, then let them go.

What are your thoughts right now? Are lots of past incidents coming into your mind? Let them go. Bring yourself back to the now by breathing deeply and relax.

The past is gone, there is nothing you can do to change it. The future is yet to come, and you cannot live it yet. There is only today, so enjoy it and do not waste a precious moment.

The only change you should be trying to make is to yourself. To make yourself better than you were the day before. There is no competition with others, only with yourself.

Every day you should strive to learn more, to love and care more, to contribute to the betterment of the world you live in and those around you.

Cause no harm to yourself, or others, or any living creature.

Breathe deeply and relax.

If you lose someone close, of course that will make you sad. Acknowledge the emotion you feel; it is natural to feel loss.

That is the main thought when someone dies, that things will never be the same again, that your life will change without them. That is perfectly true – but it can still be a good life.

You need to decide whether you want to remember this person only with sadness, or to remember them with happiness and all the laughter and good times you shared.

What a lovely way to be remembered: to always bring a smile to someone's face when they think of you, instead of a tear.

You can go on to do the best you can with your life in their memory. Helping others along the way, in memory of those we loved, is a fitting tribute to a loved one. How much better this will be, than hiding away and feeling sorry for yourself.

Has tension crept back into your body at the thought of those you have lost? If so, take a moment and use the relaxing technique used previously to relax your whole body. Be aware of your thoughts, and let tension and any negativity go.

Breathe and relax.

Your emotions are a good indicator of where your thoughts are.

Always be alert to how you feel. This will alert you to what you are actually thinking about at the moment.

Tension in the body is another indicator your thoughts are not positive. If you are about to run a race, then tension is understandable as the body prepares to run. If you are tense otherwise, ask yourself why? How many races are you running?

Where is the tension? Is it in your stomach, your neck, your chest? Wherever it is, breathe into this area. And as you breathe out, let it relax, and help your mind relax by concentrating on your breathing.

The body and mind are connected. One affects the other, so you need to be aware of thoughts and feelings if you want to regain control of your life.

Breathe deeply and relax.

YOU
and Life & Money

B reathe deeply and relax.

If you have lots of worries, ask yourself if there is something you can do to improve the situation. If the answer is 'yes', then take the action required.

Do not be afraid to face things which you feel frighten you. You will probably find that it is not as scary as you had let yourself imagine. Again, your negative thoughts have been working overtime, making you afraid.

If the answer is 'no' and you cannot do anything about what is worrying you, then stop wasting your time worrying. It won't change the situation, and you will have lost precious time which you could have spent being happier.

Always be grateful for what you have. Water, food, shelter, health, clothing, love, everything you need. Do you take all these things for granted, never notic-ing your basic needs are being met? Do you really appreciate each day and how good it is to have these things? Think every day of all the things you have to be grateful for, and give thanks.

Breathe deeply and relax. Let any tension go.

If you have debts, take action to deal with them. Even if it is only a small step, it is at least something to acknowledge you are in control. Don't think about debt all the time, or about not having enough money. That just makes the situation continue, and draws more of the same to you.

It may be that as a child you were told negative things about money, eg. money is evil, or you don't deserve to have money. Or perhaps you thought money was hard to come by as you watched your parents struggle to make ends meet. These are more limiting beliefs which you carry in your subconscious and which prevent you from living the life of abundance you are meant to have. You need to change your limiting beliefs.

Remember to repeat your affirmations and visualisation, to help positive emotion become part of your subconscious and over-ride previous negative beliefs.

The affirmations must always be in the present

tense. For example, I always have enough money; money comes to me easily and frequently. Try to feel what it would be like to have all the money you need. Use your imagination to visualise the kind of life you would live.

If you feel happy and grateful with what you have, then you will attract more into your life. You have the right to wealth; there is enough in this world for everyone. But you will be surprised how little money you need to enjoy a good life.

Breathe deeply and relax.

Do you want to have lots more money in your life? Ask yourself 'why'? Is it to feed the family and pay the bills, or is it for accumulating material possessions to boast about? Is it for prestige and power?

Money is not evil. It is what it is used for that can change it from a positive means – to bring comfort into your life and be charitable to others – to a negative means – trying to control others, or belittle those who have less than you.

Being rich does not make you a better person, or guarantee you happiness, or give you the right to look down on others. Happiness is a mindset that comes from contentment with life and being able to do good things for others. It is not governed by how much wealth you have.

Breathe deeply and relax.

YOU
and Power & Responsibility

B reathe deeply and relax.

If you have a position of power, ask yourself what are you doing with this power?

You can have power over others as a brother, sister, parent, carer, teacher, manager, in government; in fact, any position where you have influence over someone else.

With power comes great responsibility.

It should only be used to help and care for others and the world we live in. Don't use it as a weapon to bring others down, or just to make yourself feel good. Otherwise, you will feel empty inside and be continually searching for something to fill the space. This can result in you continually hurting people – mentally or physically – or depriving people of their rights, making them miserable, all just to try and make yourself happy. You will never find true happiness this way, nor will you gain the love and respect of others.

Do you constantly want more of material things? Is more never enough? Do you continually gather more material possessions and wealth, even if it means you deliberately deprive others, simply because you don't know how to be really happy?

Breathe deeply and relax.

It is not just poor people who feel unhappy. Too much money can make you miserable, just as too little can.

Perhaps deep down you feel you are not good enough, that you don't deserve happiness. Or perhaps you think you are better than everyone else and they should all serve you.

Again, these are your limiting beliefs. You have let your thoughts take control and have lost touch with the person you should be. You have let yourself become addicted to money, wealth and power, just as surely as turning to over-indulgence in alcohol, drugs, sex, or food. You are trying to use these things to blank out your life for just a few moments of pleasure. The more you give in to cravings, the more addicted you become.

Remember: a craving starts as a thought, and a thought can only become action if you let it.

You attract into your life everything you think about, so why let negative thoughts bring misery into your life? It's your mind, so always be aware of what you are thinking and only allow positive thoughts; think about the good things in life that will truly make you happy.

True happiness comes from caring for others and making the world a better place.

Every life is to be respected, be it human or animal.

Sharing your wealth makes it worthwhile. Using it to do good things will bring more happiness and contentment into your life.

Where are your thoughts now? Have they wandered away again? Let your body relax, concentrate on your breathing and let your mind become calm.

Breathe deeply and relax.

Allow your true self to emerge from deep within, and you will find the peace you crave. You have the power within to overcome anything. You don't need external stimulants. Stop thinking you do, because a thought can't do anything unless you let it. It is just a thought. And you can change your thoughts.

Only act on positive thoughts. You are stronger than you know. Think of how you truly want your life to be. What do you really want? Picture it clearly in your mind. You just have to believe in yourself. You can start right now to make the life you truly want. The first step is to believe you can do it.

Breathe deeply and relax.

If you are continually sad or angry, you are holding onto negative thoughts. Perhaps you think this is all rubbish and nothing is going to make your life better, especially not saying affirmations and thinking things will get better. Who told you it will not work? Where is your proof? What harm can thinking positively do?

Isn't it better to praise yourself than to insult yourself? Isn't it better to help others rather than put people down all the time? Or are you afraid of the difference to your life that change would make?

Some people are so afraid of change that they would rather stay in the unhappy place they are in, than step out of the routine of life as they know it. Are you one of them?

Ask yourself, do you really want to change your life? If the answer is 'no', then close the book and go back to your present life. If the answer is 'yes', then be brave and take that first step and follow what these words are saying to you.

Breathe deeply and relax.

Be brave Little one x

YOU
Can Let Go Of
Limiting Beliefs

Photograph courtesy of Pete Markham

Learn to love and believe in yourself and the amazing body and mind you have. If you choose to always feel miserable about your situation and envy others, you will attract more of the same.

You are a social being along with the billions of others on this planet. You are never really alone, even if you live alone. You flourish with love and friendship in your life.

If you are always pushing people away, it could be limiting beliefs acting on your subconscious. You need to change the way you think. Use affirmations, eg. I am a wonderful human being who attracts the love of others; I am worthy of the love that surrounds me. Feel it, believe it.

Smile at others and say hello.

Look for the good in people and you will find it.

Look for the good in yourself and stop putting yourself down. When you truly accept yourself, you will find you attract others to you. A genuine smile makes you attractive.

People will be happy to spend time with you if you are happy and caring and give out positive vibes.

Breathe deeply and relax.

Be aware of how you are feeling, as emotions are a good indicator of what you are thinking.

What are you feeling right now? Do you feel tension anywhere in your body?

Find where you feel tense and breathe deeply into this area. Let the tension leave your body, as you breathe out. Repeat this until you find there is no longer any tension.

Relax. Relax. Relax. From the top of your head to the tip of your toes, let your tension go.

YOU
and Health

Breathe deeply and relax.

If you are always negative, stressed and tense, you are inviting ill health into your body. Negativity and stress weakens your immune system, which is your body's natural defence system.

Don't dwell on aches and pains and ill health.

Some people relish ill health and love talking about all the different ailments they have experienced, drawing more ill health to them.

This again could be from learning this behaviour as a child, as more attention was given when you were ill. The more you think about ill health and talk about it, the more you attract to yourself.

You need to believe you are fit and healthy. Feel how good it feels.

Repeat your affirmation for health, eg. you have a fit, healthy body, mind and immune system. And believe it. Repeat it until it sinks into your subconscious.

Take the steps necessary to look after your body the best you can.

Breathe deeply and relax.

Many people have overcome ill health simply because they believed strongly enough that they could. Medical professionals will tell you of amazing recoveries that they can't explain, other than the patient themselves believed they would get better.

You may be one of the many people who are researching ways to find medicines to help ailments in humans and animals. You can achieve this without causing suffering, by not experimenting on living creatures who cannot volunteer for such work.

You may have a physical disability, loss of hearing, sight, or mobility. Whatever it is, this is you. We are all different in some way. Accept the way you are, you are still an amazing person.

Don't listen to anyone who tries to put you down, suggesting you are less than they are just because they think they are perfect. No-one is perfect, we all have flaws.

You have to love yourself as you are. You are unique, one of a kind, as everyone in this world is. Concentrate on all the things you can do. You can do more than other people think. You can lead a happy, successful life. Do not let anyone tell you otherwise.

Breathe deeply and relax.

YOU

and Food & Exercise

B reathe deeply and relax

You know your body will thrive on good food and exercise every day, but do you follow this?

Do your thoughts get in the way of caring for your body the way you should? Do you under or over-eat?

You need food only to sustain your body enough to live.

In moderation, food can be used for family time, socialising and sharing with others. Food should not become a force of control in your life or take over your every thought.

TV can be adding to your problem. We are inundated with adverts about food, and there are more cookery programmes day after day. Switching off the TV may be your first steps to losing weight.

Food should be as fresh and wholesome as possible, as your body prefers non processed foods, without additives and chemicals.

Challenge yourself and try making your own meals, instead of buying ready-made meals or takeaways.

Try cutting out, or cutting down, on meat and dairy products. You can live without them, as millions of people do daily. Why cuddle some animals yet stick your fork in others? Why contribute to animal suffering just to satisfy your tastebuds?

Breathe deeply and relax.

Overeating usually stems from looking for comfort that is missing from your life. If you are constantly telling yourself you can't lose weight and thinking you will always be fat, you will attract more of the same into your life. Again, hidden limiting beliefs are at work. Have affirmations ready to repeat to yourself each day, eg. I have a beautiful, fit body; I always eat a healthy diet; I enjoy exercise, etc.

Visualise and feel what it is like to be the weight you want to be. Find an exercise that you enjoy doing and fits into your daily routine. It can be walking, dancing, or working out at the gym. It can be on your own or with others. But it has to be an exercise you are drawn to and will enjoy, something you look forward to taking part in.

Try something different. There are many forms of exercise, some you may never have heard of like Pilates, Qigong, or Tai Chi.

Some people gain nothing from going to the gym and would benefit more from dancing, cycling, hiking, or team sports like football, netball, basketball, etc.

You are never too old. Start your own team if there isn't one for your age group. It is all about fun and exercise and feeling good.

Breathe deeply and relax.

The same actions can be followed if you are someone who won't eat. You are obviously unhappy, and refusing food gives you a feeling of control in your life. Again, your thoughts have become stuck in a negative view of your body. Only you can change your thoughts.

You may feel afraid of letting go of the only control you feel you have in your life. But only by being brave and changing your thoughts to food, can you regain real control. You know things can get better.

Every day repeat your own affirmations, of how you want your life to be. Really believe and feel them, and your life will get better, eg. I enjoy a healthy diet; I can eat anything I want and always maintain a healthy weight.

You deserve happiness. You are a wonderful person, worthy of love and abundance in your life. You are beautiful, and do not let your thoughts tell you anything else.

Let the past go. Today is now as good a time as any to get your thoughts under control. No-one else is to blame for you not eating, only you.

No matter what someone may have said or done to you in the past, that is where it is – in the past.

You are the one who decides to continue to let the past affect you, instead of moving on and letting go. You can change your thoughts and actions. You are stronger than you know.

To begin your journey to a better life, start by taking that first small step of accepting you can do it.

Breathe deeply and relax.

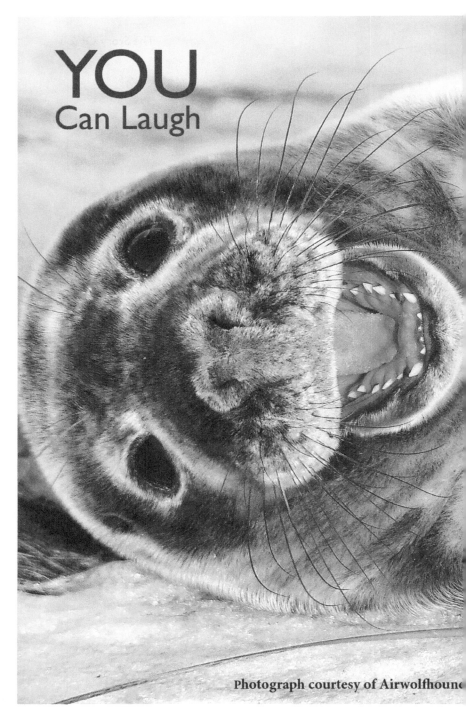

YOU
Can Laugh

Photograph courtesy of Airwolfhound

B reathe deeply and relax.

Laughter is great for healing the body and mind. Never be embarrassed to laugh in front of others.

A good hearty laugh gives the body a workout. The chemicals released in the body during laughter are therapeutic.

Try finding things every day that make you laugh. Watch funny films, or videos on the internet of people or children laughing. A baby's chuckle is really infectious.

If you can't find what makes you laugh, then act out a laugh and keep it going as long as you can. The body will not know the difference; just laugh and you will release the right chemicals in the brain to improve you mentally and physically for the better. Really go for it and laugh out loud. See if you can manage at least fifteen minutes of laughter.

Try acting laughter with friends. Join a laughter group. Sometimes it is best to be with others, as one can set the other off and before you know it, it becomes real laughter. Learn to laugh and smile every day, and encourage others to do the same. Laughter truly is the best medicine and should be prescribed daily to everyone.

Breathe deeply, relax and smile.

YOU
Need to use
Positive Words
& Forgiveness

B reathe deeply and relax.

Learn to avoid gossip and always say positive things to others.

Think about what people are actually saying to you. Sometimes you can pick things up wrong, as you haven't really understood what the other person is trying to say. Not everyone is gifted at getting what they really mean across to others, and this can lead to ill feeling because the words used were not clear, or came out wrong.

We all see things from our own viewpoint. You and a friend could be approaching each other on the same street. If you were both asked to describe what you could see on your right hand side, you would both give different descriptions, but you would still be on the same street.

Try to see the world through the eyes of others; you might be surprised to find you really are on the same side.

Breathe deeply and relax. Let any tension go.

Learn to forgive. You don't have to condone a wrong action by someone towards you, but you can forgive by letting it go and not dwelling on it, as it will only lead to more unhappiness for you.

Do not let past hurts play over and over in your mind.

Change your thoughts by finding a good memory.

Think of something that makes you smile, really see it in your mind and really feel the happiness connected to this memory. Then press your thumbs and forefinger together for a few minutes while the thought is there.

You can then use this anytime bad memories come into your head; simply press your thumbs and forefingers together, and with practice this should bring the good memory back instead.

Breathe deeply and relax.

Stop continually looking for the worst in people, and try to see their good points instead. By concentrating on their good points, your attitude to others will change and you may find their attitude to you will also change.

Finding fault in others is usually because you don't feel good about yourself, and often the faults you see in others are reflections of your own faults. Always be aware of how you speak and act towards others. We are all here to care for each other. Your words and actions can help others to see this and to help the world become a better place for everyone.

Breathe deeply and relax.

YOU
Can Prevent
Limiting Beliefs

Photograph courtesy of Thomas Leth-Olsen

B reathe deeply and relax.

You must prevent creating limiting beliefs in others, especially your children, or any children you come into contact with.

Be aware of how you speak and the words you use. Be positive and praise children often. Do not harm them in any way, mentally or physically. Use kind words and actions to help them learn. Children should be brought up with love and be protected by everyone.

If you are a child, do not let others fill you with limiting beliefs. Do not let insults stay in your mind and do not use insults to others. Do not pick on others because they are different.

Everyone is different, including you. Everyone is special, and you should enjoy and marvel at all the similarities or differences between yourself and others.

Breathe and relax, and let any tension go.

Help all children to keep their imagination. Let no-one crush their dreams. Encourage their wonder in the world and teach them to be kind and caring to all and everything.

Children should learn about the mind, how to change their thoughts from negative to positive ones, and to be aware of their emotions.

Teach them to breathe deeply and relax, and be aware of their thoughts.

Children should be allowed to learn at their own pace, and in the way that suits their particular abilities.

Parents and carers should tell children each day that they are loved and special and can achieve anything they want to be.

Guide them and help them learn the difference between right and wrong.

Let them learn how to be truly happy, to care for others and the world in which they live, and to reach their full potential.

Children are the future of this world.

Breathe deeply and relax.

Do not criticise others and constantly point out their faults. Help them to find the positive things about themselves. This includes how you talk and think about yourself. For remember: what you think about, you bring about.

YOU

The World & Opportunites

Photograph courtesy of Gino Sta.maria

B reathe deeply and relax.

You live in a world where everyone is trying to be happy, but not everyone knows the right way to go about this.

You will hear people putting others down to make themselves feel they are better than the person they insult. They will try to get you to join in, so they feel they are part of some kind of righteous group with everyone against the other person. Do not travel this road. You will only draw in unhappiness to yourself, as well as to the other person.

If you are the victim, do not strike back with more insults. Do not let unhappy thoughts take hold, but remind yourself you have the power not to let negative words affect you. Remember the person who insults another is trying to make themself feel good; he or she has lost the way to their own happiness and will only attract more unhappiness to themself.

Do not let yourself be imprisoned by what other people say. Let their words go and be free.

Breathe deeply and relax.

Never set out to harm anyone, or any living thing.

Next time you chase a wild animal from your garden, remember it was their garden first.

You will only bring suffering to yourself by hurting any sentient being.

Never be responsible for causing pain and suffering, unless you want to attract more of the same into your life.

You live on this earth and have a responsibility to protect it as best you can.

The earth was here before you, and will be here after you have gone. You are just a visitor and, like all good visitors, you should take care of your host's home. Make sure you do not leave a mess or damage.

You should appreciate the privilege you have to be part of this wonderful world and enjoy the beauty and abundance it provides.

Your country and your people are no better, or worse, than any other countries and their people.

Every life has the same value. Everyone is a visitor to this planet and all are equal, no matter the colour of your skin, whether you are male or female. No-one has the right to dominate another.

Breathe deeply and relax.

Really appreciate nature and the wonderful world you live in. It is time to appreciate and care for all that surrounds you, to really look closely, not just see with a token glance of the eyes, but to really look at all that surrounds you.

Look at all the wonders and beauty that nature provides – the mountains, hills, seas, and different landscapes. The variety of flowers and trees, the birds and animals, to the tiniest insects. Marvel at and respect them all. They each have their right to be on this planet.

Take time to appreciate and marvel at the skills of human craftsmanship, from the buildings that surround us to the technology that is everywhere, the cars and planes, the very cup we drink from, and the table we put it on.

All of these things started with a thought in someone's mind. Someone who believed they could achieve, and did. These people did not allow any failures to stand in their way of success.

Failures are how we learn. They show us another way of how not to do something. And the more you try and don't give up, you will find the right way to succeed.

Every invention still to come is out there just waiting for someone to make the thought reality. It could be you, if you believe in yourself strongly enough and acknowledge your intuition.

How often have you had a thought or feeling urging you on to do something, but you have thought 'I can't do that. I am not clever enough'? Maybe you put it off to tomorrow, or next week. Or maybe you felt frightened, because it would mean changing your life. Or you let someone else talk you out of it, and so the idea left your mind along with the chance you had to do something great.

Learn to follow your gut feelings, your intuition. Everyone is born with it, but perhaps you have learned to suppress it at some point in your life and just need to acknowledge it again.

Be alert to all around you, and grasp at the chances that come into your life. As you are learning to think positively and believe in yourself, more chances are going to come into your life. Be ready to recognise them and act to change your world.

Where are your thoughts now? Bring them back to now and breathe deeply and relax.

YOU
and Challenges

Breathe deeply and relax.

Even when you are being positive, things you don't want can happen in life, because we share this world with many others. Look on these moments, not as obstacles in your way, but as challenges to be overcome and you will always find a way.

Set yourself little goals every day.

Step out of your normal routine. Take the bus instead of the car. Get off the bus a stop earlier and enjoy the extra walk.

If you have a job, go for a walk at lunch time, or in the evening.

Learn something new.

Visit somewhere you have never been before.

Give some time to help others.

Do something to show the people you love how you feel about them.

Walk your dog a different route, or walk someone else's dog if you don't have one.

Try growing your own fruit or vegetables. If you have no garden, use some pots.

Write a poem, a song, a book, a play. Paint or draw a picture. Let your imagination run free.

Breathe deeply and relax.

Do not hide away and be afraid of facing each day. Things will never change if you do. Instead, face up to each day and appreciate you have an opportunity to make your life better.

You will be surprised how many people are around you who will be willing to help you get back on your feet. The world is a wonderful place, and you just have to open your eyes and regain control of your thoughts to see this.

You are the master of you. There is no limit to what you can do, other than the limits you set yourself.

Always remember to breathe deeply and relax, and always be aware of your thoughts and feelings.

YOU

Photograph courtesy of Tim Green

You are the only one who will live your story to the end.

May you have a happy, fulfilling journey.

About The Author

Sheila Griffiths was born and brought up in Scotland, the youngest of five children and the only girl. She is now a mother of three and has two grand daughters. For many years she has been interested in the mind and gained an honours degree in psychology. She has developed a lot of life experience through her work as a nursery nurse, in Social Work and elderly care and her voluntary roles in victim support and coaching gymnastics.

Sheila has connected with many people over the years who were going through difficult periods in their lives and witnessed how the mind plays a big part in how people responded. This encouraged her to develop her research further in meditation and the benefits it can bring. Sheila has found it is the simple things that help people the most and shares her findings with others in this her first book. If you have any comments on this book please contact Sheila : primapj@yahoo.com